GOOD-BYE SKINK

Psychoanalytic Thought for Youth

GOOD-BYE SKINK

By Suzanne T. Saldarini

Illustrated by Lou Simeone

To my children:

Charles Thomas

Shelley

John Christopher

Published in 2019 by ORI Academic Press,
New York, NY

Copyright © 2018 by Suzanne T. Saldarini
All rights reserved.

For permissions to reproduce more than 300 words of this publication, email to ORIPressEditor@Gmail.com or write to ORI Academic Press Editor @ 7515 187th St, Fresh Meadows, NY 11366.

Printed in the United States of America on acid free paper.

Library of Congress Control Number: 2019936909

Cataloging Data:

Saldarini, Suzanne T. GOOD-BYE SKINK / Suzanne T. Saldarini

1. Family & Relationships / Death, Grief, Bereavement. 2. Psychology / Developmental / Child. 3. Self-Help / Communication & Social Skills.

ISBN-13: 978-1-942431-13-8 (color paperback)

Illustrations - by Lou Simeone @ simeonegraphix.com.

Book design and editing - by MindMendMedia, Inc. @ www.MindMendMedia.com.

PUBLISHER'S PREFACE

"Granny, will you die? Soon? Great! That's when I finally will use your sewing machine!"

(Korney Chukovsky, *From Two to Five*)

Suzanne Saldarini did it again – she offered us another brilliant book, and this time, it is about one of the most difficult (and often taboo) topics encountered by those who care for children. *Good-bye Skink* is about an inescapable part of life – death, and how to explain it to young children. Suzanne Saldarini explains it honestly, normalizing the array of emotional reactions a child might have to the death of a loved one, a person or a pet.

Following in the footsteps of Mr. Rogers, Suzanne allows the children "to be," to express their grief reactions when the classroom pet Skink dies – from denial to regression, from anger to acceptance, and finally, to the memories of their pet Skink, silly or sad, and to celebration of the joys that Skink brought to these children's lives when it was alive.

This book is very timely. With the development of Internet-based gaming, death is portrayed as something reversible or temporary, not real and impersonal. Some young children have an idea of their omnipotence (never dying), while others are ridden with fears and anxieties about their loved ones dying (and possibly leaving them alone in this big cold world). All children ask questions about death sometime in their early years, and their reactions are based on the level of their development and on their experiences with death, and how it was explained by adults. *Good-bye Skink* serves as a kind preparation for such conversation.

As in her other books for children (published by ORI Academic Press), Suzanne Saldarini does not preach or lecture, and she does not restrict the reader's imagination; quite the opposite – while reading this book, children are offered to share "the news" and to show their own and their families' reactions to various life events. The text of the story is beautifully illustrated and complemented by engaging fun activity pages too.

At ORI Academic Press, we are delighted to be a part of *Good-bye Skink* story, which – we are sure – will be appreciated by everyone who needs to open the conversation about processing grief and loss in kids, without any one-size-fits-all assumptions and expectations.

Dr. Inna Rozentsvit,\
on behalf of ORI Academic Press

AUTHOR'S INTRODUCTION: A CAUTIONARY TALE

Many years ago, when I was a graduate student at the University of Kansas, the Department of Human Development included a Nursery School; the school served as a laboratory for their graduate students – for those in Education and for those, like me, in Psychology. As candidates, we had opportunities to serve there as Teaching Assistants. Assistants interacted with the children and prepared play areas. We filled paint pots for Easel Painting, tidied Dress-Up and Housekeeping, arranged scissors, glue, paper and attractive odds and ends on the Collage Table, checked stacks of unit blocks, cared for small pets etc. etc. etc. We did not direct play, but "floated" through play spaces offering support, observations and invitations as needed. Located in a rambling old house at the top of a grassy hill the school had spacious rooms and a large outdoor play area. The optimistic, permissive air of the 1960's Human Potential movement hung about the place – I loved it. The children were challenging and adorable; our Head Teacher, Carolyn, was brilliant. I added my toddler son's name to the school's waiting list.

One morning, as I passed by the terrarium, I noticed that our usually energetic Skink was oddly motionless. I poked it experimentally and then picked it up. It was quite stiff – the little animal was clearly dead.

"Now what?" I fretted, "What does one do with a dead Skink?" The terrarium was a popular site; I was sure the children would be frightened and shocked by the sight of a dead creature. I had no idea what to say.

Then, my eye caught a large covered trash bin. Just as I was poised to deposit the Skink in that bin, Carolyn approached.

"What are you doing?" she asked.

"It's the Skink," I explained, "It is dead."

"And what will you tell the children?" she asked. "How will you explain where it is? If you say it is dead, will you say dead things go in the trash?"

Putting the Skink in the trash now seemed cowardly and indefensible… "Let's put it back in the terrarium," said Carolyn, "Sit near-by and watch the children's reactions – try and help them understand."

And so the Good-bye Skink morning developed. The children were curious as ever, and also disappointed, sad, disbelieving, lost, and even angry. Most seemed unsure of what "dead" meant, but none were shocked or frightened as I had feared. Clearly, the most uncomfortable feelings in the room belonged to me; my initial worries about "what to say" masked a deeper wish to avoid recognition of that undeniable and unpleasant reality, death.

Years passed. I'm not sure what the children learned that morning, but memory of Skink moments became a kind of cautionary tale for me. When I've been too quick to sooth a patient's anxious feelings, or too skilled at softening a disturbing reality, I remember those sturdy three year olds. No one has all the "right answers" about death or countless other painful conflicts and events, but everyone can learn to acknowledge – and grow – from the challenging feelings they stir.

Teachable moments and unconscious fears acknowledged – these are tools for wide-awake helpers in both classrooms and behind analytic couches.

Suzanne Saldarini 12/13/18

GOOD-BYE SKINK

Once upon a time, in a place called Acorn School, a small brown Skink lived in a fine glass terrarium. The terrarium sat near a big sunny window. The terrarium had springy green moss and soft yellow sand on its floor; it had a flat gray rock and also a strong, tall twig.

All of this made a comfortable home for the Skink. The Skink could dig holes in the springy moss, sun itself on the flat gray rock or climb to the top of the twig and watch everything in the school.

Every day at Acorn School children brought wonderful things for the Skink to eat. Harry brought juicy strawberries – cut just right for the Skink's small jaws. Martha brought cheerios, Dora brought wiggly bugs and Peter brought lettuce. When the Skink saw children, it stood up on its hind legs, leaned against the side of the terrarium and opened its jaws as far as it could.

The Skink liked digging holes in the springy moss, it liked resting on the warm, flat rock, and it liked to climb the tall twig but most of all that Skink loved to eat!

…

One day the Skink did not run to the side of the Terrarium for Harry's strawberries. It did not stand up on its feet for Martha's cheerios, or Dora's wiggly bugs, or even for Peter's lettuce. It did not move, and its eyes were closed.

No one understood why the Skink was so still.

"I think it's tired," said Harry.
"Or maybe sleeping," said Martha.
"It's not hungry today," said Dora.
"I don't think it likes us anymore," said Peter.
Grace looked inside the terrarium; she didn't say anything…
…
Very gently, with just one finger, Harry poked the Skink. It did not move its legs, it did not move its tail, and it did not open its eyes. "Come and look at the Skink," said Harry to their teacher, Miss Anna, "It won't wake up."

Miss Anna picked the Skink up and put it in her hand. She moved each one of its front legs, she moved each one of its back legs and she moved its tail, but the Skink did not move itself.

"This Skink is not sleeping," she said to the children. "It is not alive anymore. This Skink is dead."

"Is it tired?" asked Harry. "Will it get up tomorrow?"

"No," said Miss Anna, "Dead means it will not get up tomorrow. It won't ever get up anymore."

"But what if it wants to eat cheerios?" said Dora, "What if it wants to see us?"

"The Skink can't want anymore," said Miss Anna.

Martha began to cry. "I don't want the Skink to be dead," she said.

"It is very sad for us," said Miss Anna. She put her arm around Martha, "We will all miss our Skink."

"I don't like this," said Peter in a cross voice. "I'm going to play with trucks." He walked away.

Grace put her thumb in her mouth and cuddled up to Miss Anna; she didn't say anything.

… Later, during News at Circle Time, Harry raised his hand.

"Our Skink is dead," he said. "It won't get up tomorrow," he added. "The Skink will still be dead tomorrow."

"I'm very sad," said Martha, "I cried."

Miss Anna picked up her guitar. "Maybe we can sing about our Skink," she said. She strummed a few chords.

"Poor Skink is dead," she sang,
"Poor brown Skink is dead.
Let's sing a song to make a sad good-bye.
It no longer comes to eat,
It won't stand up on its feet…"

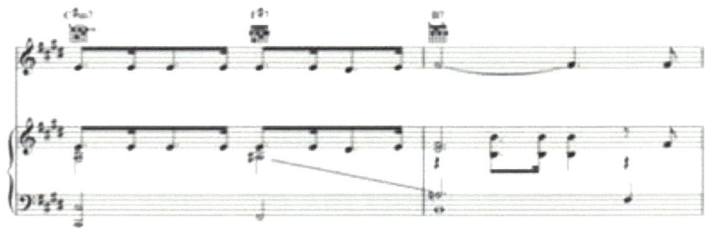

She was quiet for a minute and then asked, "Can someone add something to my song?"

"I can," said Martha. "*Oh Skink we miss you so, oh me oh my.*"

"Let's all sing," said Miss Anna.

Everyone sang the *Good-bye Skink* song together.

After singing, some of the children had more news to share.

Dora said, "My Mommy has a new friend called Jim." Martha said, "My dog Topsy has six puppies. They cry a lot."

Dora said, "And I have a rabbit at my Daddy's house. And I'm going to visit him on Sunday. And I have a sister there too. Her name is Lizzie. She is so little she can't even talk. And she didn't come from my Mommy's tummy. *I came from my Mommy's tummy.* Lizzie came from Margaret's tummy, but she's still my sister."

Miss Anna said, "Dora has lots of people to know." "Yes," said Dora, "Lots of people."

Martha looked at Grace. "Do you have news today?" she asked. "No," said Grace. She put her thumb in her mouth and looked away.

Alexander said, "Well, I have news. My Grandma and I cooked our own playdoh right in the kitchen. It was too hot to touch for a long time. I had to wait."

Miss Anna said, "Waiting is hard."

"Yes," said Alexander, "waiting is very hard."

"Oh," said Harry, "I lost my Binky last night and I had to wait 'till Daddy found it – that was hard too."

"Losing important things is very hard," said Miss Anna, "We all lost our Skink today, but we'll remember it for a long time."

And then there was even more news… Do you have news to share?

WRITE OR DRAW YOUR NEWS TO SHARE HERE:

Soon it was Outdoor Playtime. "I will put the Skink's body in a box," said Miss Anna, "We can bury it in our garden. Would anyone like to help?"

"I will," said Peter. "Let's put it by the lettuce. That Skink liked lettuce."

Peter and Miss Anna dug a hole in the garden. They put the box in the hole and covered it with dirt.

Harry watched and said, "Wait just a minute." He went inside and took the tall climbing twig and the flat rock out of the terrarium. "Here," he said to Miss Anna, "These can mark our Skink's place."

"That's called a grave," said Miss Anna. "When we see it we'll remember."

After Outdoor Playtime school was over for the day.

The children left.

When Harry got home he said, "I know what dead is."

When Peter got home he said, "I helped Miss Anna today."

When Dora got home she said, "I love News at Circle Time."

When Grace got home she said, "My tummy hurts." Grace's Mommy gave her a big hug and then they had a long talk.

…The next day Grace was first with News to Share.

"My Mommy and I made more words for the Skink song," she said, "and here they are." She gave Miss Anna a blue paper.

Miss Anna and Grace sang these words:

> *"Yesterday was sad*
> *I don't like feeling bad*
> *I didn't like so many long good-byes.*
> *Then my Mommy let me know*
> *That all feelings come and go –*
> *And words can change*
> *Gray clouds to sunny skies."*

"Let's all sing Grace's song together," said Miss Anna.
And so they did.
It was another busy day at Acorn school.

Suzanne Saldarini, Mahwah NJ

SKINK ACTIVITIES:
FUN WITH RHYMES, WORDS, AND WISHES

Good-bye, Skink!

FUN WITH RHYMES

CHOOSE A WORD TO FINISH EACH RHYME:

If you choose to draw a **SKINK**,

Make it brown and never _____

(red? yellow? pink?)

And the reason for this **RULE**?

Well, I learned it at my _____

(store? school? park?)

Skinks can move without a **TRACE**

Color makes their hiding _____

(cave? den? place?)

When they're safely out of **SIGHT**,

No hungry hunter gets a _____

(snack? meal? bite?)

So brown Skinks really stay quite **FREE**

To run through sand or climb a _ _ _ _ _ _ _ _ _ _ _ _ _

(pole? rock? tree?)

Now you can see with all this **COVER**

A Skink is not like any _ _ _ _ _ _ _ _ _ _ _ _ _ _ _

(bird? fish? other?)

MORE RHYMES

The Skink was our good **FRIEND**;

We loved it till the very _ _ _ _ _ _ _ _ _ _ _ _ _ _ _ _

(winter? summer? end?)

We wish it was still with us in our **SCHOOL**…

It is fun to have a **PET** –

It comes with chores we won't _ _ _ _ _ _ _ _ _ _ _ _ _

(remember? like? forget?)

Remembering is always a good _ _ _ _ _ _ _ _ _ _ _ _ _

(rule? thing? job?)

FUN WITH WORDS

Underline words that can change your CLOUDS to SUNNY SKIES:

YOU ARE MY FRIEND.

SIT NEXT TO ME.

I'M SORRY.

WILL YOU PLAY WITH ME?

I LOVE YOU.

WRITE YOUR OWN SUNNY WORDS HERE:

_____ _____

_____ _____

_____ _____

_____ _____

_____ _____

FUN WITH WISHES

CHOOSE A WISH:

I WISH IT WAS MY BIRTHDAY.

I WISH I HAD A PET.

I WISH I COULD RIDE A TWO-WHEEL BIKE.

WRITE YOUR OWN WISH HERE:

_____ _____

_____ _____

_____ _____

_____ _____

_____ _____

_____ _____

AFTERWORD: THOUGHTS FOR TEACHERS AND PARENTS

Some adult readers, kind enough to preview *Good-Bye Skink*, have wished for longer, more detailed and guided Circle Time discussions aimed at comforting children. I chose instead to present that part of the story as close as possible to my memory of it. That is, the teacher accepts and reflects each child's reaction, is undismayed by contributions that may initially seem off target, and then comfortably invites the group to respond together.

The agenda belongs to the children, protected, hopefully, from anxious adult expectations about what "should" be accomplished. None of this suggests that there is no place for thoughtfulness when children seek comfort and understanding. Accepting and encouraging curiosity, as well as giving verbal expression to feelings, sharing experiences and making memories – are all central to pre-school education. A classroom pet's death, while sad, is also a natural learning opportunity.

The learning objectives listed here, along with additional resources cited below, aim to help adults shape their own approach to this challenging topic:

1. Make death a safe topic for questions and discussion.

2. Distinguish death from sleep.

3. Affirm the validity of each individual's response. There is no "right way" to feel. For example, Harry responds with curiosity; Peter – with anger; Martha denies, while Dora feels an anxious sort of narcissism; and Grace regresses. Interestingly, an adult reader, a nurse, remarked that the children's reactions to Skink's death were similar to those often felt by grieving adults.

4. Observe how using words can help us express and tolerate difficult feelings.

5. Present death as a natural part of life.

6. Build empathy and community with memorials of the shared loss (songs, rituals, monuments, etc.).

ADDITIONAL RESOURCES:

Brown, Margaret Wise (1986). *The Dead Bird*. Harper Collins.

Chukovsky, K. (1963, Miriam Morton translation). *From Two to Five.* Berkeley, CA: University of California Press.

Parr, T. (2015). *The Goodbye Book.* New York, NY: Little, Brown & Company.

Rogers, F. (1998). *When a pet dies.* London, UK: Puffin / Penguin Young Readers Group.

Viorst, J. (1971). *The tenth good thing about Barney.* New York, NY: Atheneum / Simon & Schuster.

Mr. Rogers' Neighborhood (n.d.). *Mr. Rogers talks about death* [video file]. Retrieved from https://youtu.be/LDnDs1Rz4ZQ

Mr. Rogers' Neighborhood (n.d.). *Episode 1101: Death of the goldfish* [video file]. Retrieved from https://vimeo.com/153417661

*Note: Miss Anna borrowed the melody for GOOD-BYE SKINK from the song "Pore Jud" ("Oklahoma!" musical, by Rodgers and Hammerstein), but any suitably sad tune will do.

WE SAID, GOOD-BYE SKINK.
IT IS YOUR TURN NOW!

www.ingramcontent.com/pod-product-compliance
Lightning Source LLC
Chambersburg PA
CBHW042004150426
43194CB00002B/123